THE MASQUE OF PANDORA

THE MASQUE OF PANDORA

AND OTHER POEMS

BY
HENRY WADSWORTH LONGFELLOW

1875

This text was originally published in the United States
in the year 1875
The text is in the public domain.
Modern Edition © 2022
Word Well Books

The publishers have made all reasonable efforts to ensure this
book is indeed in the Public Domain in any and all territories it has been
published.

CONTENTS

THE MASQUE OF PANDORA

I.

THE WORKSHOP OF HEPHAESTUS

HEPHÆSTUS, *standing before the statue of Pandora.*

Not fashioned out of gold, like Hera's throne,
Nor forged of iron like the thunderbolts
Of Zeus omnipotent, or other works
Wrought by my hands at Lemnos or Olympus,
But moulded in soft clay, that unresisting
Yields itself to the touch, this lovely form
Before me stands perfect in every part.
Not Aphrodite's self appeared more fair,
When first upwafted by caressing winds
She came to high Olympus, and the gods
Paid homage to her beauty. Thus her hair
Was cinctured; thus her floating drapery
Was like a cloud about her, and her face
Was radiant with the sunshine and the sea.

THE VOICE OF ZEUS.

Is thy work done, Hephæstus?

HEPHÆSTUS

It is finished!

THE VOICE.

Not finished till I breathe the breath of life
Into her nostrils, and she moves and speaks.

HEPHÆSTUS.

Will she become immortal like ourselves?

THE VOICE.

The form that thou hast fashioned out of clay
Is of the earth and mortal; but the spirit,
The life, the exhalation of my breath,
Is of diviner essence and immortal.
The gods shall shower on her their benefactions,
She shall possess all gifts: the gift of song,
The gift of eloquence, the gift of beauty,
The fascination and the nameless charm
That shall lead all men captive.

HEPHÆSTUS.

Wherefore? wherefore?

A wind shakes the house.

I hear the rushing of a mighty wind
Through all the halls and chambers of my house!
Her parted lips inhale it, and her bosom
Heaves with the inspiration. As a reed
Beside a river in the rippling current
Bends to and fro, she bows or lifts her head.
She gazes round about as if amazed;
She is alive; she breathes, but yet she speaks not!

Pandora descends from the pedestal.

CHORUS OF THE GRACES.

AGLAIA.

In the workshop of Hephaestus
    What is this I see?
Have the Gods to four increased us
    Who were only three?
Beautiful in form and feature,
    Lovely as the day,
Can there be so fair a creature
    Formed of common clay?

THALIA.

O sweet, pale face! O lovely eyes of azure,
    Clear as the waters of a brook that run
    Limpid and laughing in the summer sun!
    O golden hair that like a miser's treasure
In its abundance overflows the measure!
    O graceful form, that cloudlike floatest on
    With the soft, undulating gait of one
    Who moveth as if motion were a pleasure!
By what name shall I call thee? Nymph or Muse,
    Callirrhoë or Urania? Some sweet name
    Whose every syllable is a caress
Would best befit thee; but I cannot choose,
    Nor do I care to choose; for still the same,
    Nameless or named, will be thy loveliness.

EUPHROSYNE.

Dowered with all celestial gifts,
    Skilled in every art
That ennobles and uplifts
    And delights the heart,
Fair on earth shall be thy fame
    As thy face is fair,
And Pandora be the name
    Thou henceforth shalt bear.

II.

OLYMPUS

HERMES, *putting on his sandals.*

MUCH must he toil who serves the Immortal Gods,
And I, who am their herald, most of all.
No rest have I, nor respite. I no sooner
Unclasp the winged sandals from my feet,
Than I again must clasp them, and depart
Upon some foolish errand. But to-day
The errand is not foolish. Never yet
With greater joy did I obey the summons
That sends me earthward. I will fly so swiftly
That my caduceus in the whistling air
Shall make a sound like the Pandæan pipes,
Cheating the shepherds; for to-day I go,
Commissioned by high-thundering Zeus, to lead
A maiden to Prometheus, in his tower,
And by my cunning arguments persuade him
To marry her. What mischief lies concealed
In this design I know not; but I know
Who thinks of marrying hath already taken
One step upon the road to penitence.
Such embassies delight me. Forth I launch
On the sustaining air, nor fear to fall
 Like Icarus, nor swerve aside like him
Who drove amiss Hyperion's fiery steeds.
 I sink, I fly! The yielding element
Folds itself round about me like an arm,
And holds me as a mother holds her child.

III.

TOWER OF PROMETHEUS
ON MOUNT CAUCASUS

PROMETHEUS.

I hear the trumpet of Alectryon
Proclaim the dawn. The stars begin to fade,
And all the heavens are full of prophecies
And evil auguries. Blood-red last night
I saw great Kronos rise; the crescent moon
Sank through the mist, as if it were the scythe
His parricidal hand had flung far down
The western steeps. O ye Immortal Gods,
What evil are ye plotting and contriving?

HERMES *and* PANDORA *at the threshold.*

PANDORA.

I cannot cross the threshold. An unseen
And icy hand repels me. These blank walls
Oppress me with their weight!

PROMETHEUS.

          Powerful ye are,
But not omnipotent. Ye cannot fight
Against Necessity. The Fates control you,
As they do us, and so far we are equals!

PANDORA.

Motionless, passionless, companionless,
He sits there muttering in his beard. His voice
Is like a river flowing underground!

HERMES.

Prometheus, hail!

PROMETHEUS.

Who calls me?

HERMES.

       It is I.
Dost thou not know me?

PROMETHEUS.

      By thy winged cap
And winged heels I know thee. Thou art Hermes,
Captain of thieves! Hast thou again been stealing
The heifers of Admetus in the sweet
Meadows of asphodel? or Hera's girdle?
Or the earth-shaking trident of Poseidon?

HERMES.

And thou, Prometheus; say, hast thou again
Been stealing fire from Helios' chariot-wheels
To light thy furnaces?

PROMETHEUS.

Why comest thou hither
So early in the dawn?

HERMES.

The Immortal Gods
Know naught of late or early. Zeus himself
The omnipotent hath sent me.

PROMETHEUS.

For what purpose?

HERMES.

To bring this maiden to thee.

PROMETHEUS.

I mistrust
The Gods and all their gifts. If they have sent her
It is for no good purpose.

HERMES.

What disaster
Could she bring on thy house, who is a woman?

PROMETHEUS.

The Gods are not my friends, nor am I theirs.
Whatever comes from them, though in a shape
As beautiful as this, is evil only.
Who art thou?

PANDORA.

       One who, though to thee unknown,
Yet knoweth thee.

PROMETHEUS.

       How shouldst thou know me, woman?

PANDORA.

Who knoweth not Prometheus the humane?

PROMETHEUS.

Prometheus the unfortunate; to whom
Both Gods and men have shown themselves ungrateful.
When every spark was quenched on every hearth
Throughout the earth, I brought to man the fire
And all its ministrations. My reward
Hath been the rock and vulture.

HERMES.

       But the Gods
At last relent and pardon.

PROMETHEUS.

They relent not;
They pardon not; they are implacable,
Revengeful, unforgiving!

HERMES.

As a pledge
Of reconciliation they have sent to thee
This divine being, to be thy companion,
And bring into thy melancholy house
The sunshine and the fragrance of her youth.

PROMETHEUS.

I need them not. I have within myself
All that my heart desires; the ideal beauty
Which the creative faculty of mind
Fashions and follows in a thousand shapes
More lovely than the real. My own thoughts
Are my companions; my designs and labors
And aspirations are my only friends.

HERMES.

Decide not rashly. The decision made
Can never be recalled. The Gods implore not,
Plead not, solicit not; they only offer
Choice and occasion, which once being passed
Return no more. Dost thou accept the gift?

PROMETHEUS.

No gift of theirs, in whatsoever shape
It comes to me, with whatsoever charm
To fascinate my sense, will I receive.
Leave me.

PANDORA.

Let us go hence. I will not stay.

HERMES.

We leave thee to thy vacant dreams, and all
The silence and the solitude of thought,
The endless bitterness of unbelief,
The loneliness of existence without love.

CHORUS OF THE FATES.

CLOTHO.

How the Titan, the defiant,
The self-centred, self-reliant,
Wrapped in visions and illusions,
Robs himself of life's best gifts!
Till by all the storm-winds shaken,
By the blast of fate o'ertaken,
Hopeless, helpless, and forsaken
In the mists of his confusions
To the reefs of doom he drifts!

LACHESIS.

Sorely tried and sorely tempted,
From no agonies exempted,
In the penance of his trial,
And the discipline of pain;
Often by illusions cheated,
Often baffled and defeated
In the tasks to be completed,
He, by toil and self-denial,
To the highest shall attain.

ATROPOS.

Tempt no more the noble schemer;
Bear unto some idle dreamer
This new toy and fascination,
This new dalliance and delight!
To the garden where reposes
Epimetheus crowned with roses,
To the door that never closes
Upon pleasure and temptation,
Bring this vision of the night!

IV.

THE AIR

HERMES, *returning to Olympus.*

As lonely as the tower that he inhabits,
As form and cold as are the crags about him,
Prometheus stands. The thunderbolts of Zeus
Alone can move him; but the tender heart
Of Epimetheus, burning at white heat,
Hammers and flames like all his brother's forges!
Now as an arrow from Hyperion's bow,
My errand done, I fly, I float, I soar
Into the air returning to Olympus.
O joy of motion! O delight to cleave
The infinite realms of space, the liquid ether,
Through the warm sunshine and the cooling cloud,
Myself as light as sunbeam or as cloud!
With one touch of my swift and winged feet,
I spurn the solid earth, and leave it rocking
As rocks the bough from which a bird takes wing.

V.

THE HOUSE OF EPIMETHEUS

EPIMETHEUS.

BEAUTIFUL apparition! go not hence !
Surely thou art a Goddess, for thy voice
Is a celestial melody, and thy form
Self-poised as if it floated on the air!

PANDORA.

No Goddess am I, nor of heavenly birth,
But a mere woman fashioned out of clay
And mortal as the rest.

EPIMETHEUS.

       Thy face is fair;
There is a wonder in thine azure eyes
That fascinates me. thy whole presence seems
A soft desire, a breathing thought of love.
Say, would thy star like Merope's grow dim
If thou shouldst wed beneath thee?

PANDORA.

       Ask me not;
I cannot answer thee. I only know
The Gods have sent me hither.

EPIMETHEUS.

   I believe,
And thus believing am most fortunate.
It was not Hermes led thee here, but Eros,
And swifter than his arrows were thine eyes
In wounding me. There was no moment's space
Between my seeing thee and loving thee.
O, what a tell-tale face thou hast ! Again
I see the wonder in thy tender eyes.

PANDORA.

They do but answer to the love in thine,
Yet secretly I wonder thou shouldst love me.
Thou knowest me not.

EPIMETHEUS.

     Perhaps I know thee better
Than had I known thee longer. Yet it seems
That I have always known thee, and but now
Have found thee. Ah, I have been waiting long.

PANDORA.

How beautiful is this house! The atmosphere
Breathes rest and comfort, and the many chambers
Seem full of welcomes.

EPIMETHEUS.

          They not only seem,
But truly are. This dwelling and its master \
Belong to thee.

PANDORA.

          Here let me stay forever!
There is a spell upon me.

EPIMETHEUS.

          Thou thyself
Art the enchantress, and I feel thy power
Envelop me, and wrap my soul and sense
In an Elysian dream.

PANDORA.

          O, let me stay.
How beautiful are all things round about me,
Multiplied by the mirrors on the walls!
What treasures hast thou here! Yon oaken chest,
Carven with figures and embossed with gold,
Is wonderful to look upon! What choice
And precious things dost thou keep hidden in it?

EPIMETHEUS.

I know not. 'Tis a mystery.

PANDORA

Hast thou never
Lifted the lid?

EPIMETHEUS.

The oracle forbids.
Safely concealed there from all mortal eyes
Forever sleeps the secret of the Gods.
Seek not to know what they have hidden from thee,
Till they themselves reveal it.

PANDORA.

As thou wilt.

EPIMETHEUS.

Let us go forth from this mysterious place.
The garden walks are pleasant at this hour;
The nightingales among the sheltering boughs
Of populous and many-nested trees
Shall teach me how to woo thee, and shall tell me
By what resistless charms or incantations
They won their mates.

PANDORA.

Thou dost not need a teacher.

They go out.

CHORUS OF THE EUMENIDES.

What the Immortals
Confide to thy keeping,
Tell unto no man;
Waking or sleeping,
Closed be thy portals
To friend as to foeman.

Silence conceals it;
The word that is spoken
Betrays and reveals it;
By breath or by token
The charm may be broken.

With shafts of their splendors
The Gods unforgiving
Pursue the offenders,
The dead and the living!
Fortune forsakes them,
Nor earth shall abide them,
Nor Tartarus hide them;
Swift wrath overtakes 'them!

With useless endeavor,
Forever, forever,
Is Sisyphus rolling
His stone up the mountain!
Immersed in the fountain,
Tantalus tastes not
The water that wastes not!
Through ages increasing
The pangs that afflict him,
With motion unceasing
The wheel of Ixion
Shall torture its victim!

VI.

IN THE GARDEN

EPIMETHEUS.

YON snow-white cloud that sails sublime in ether
Is but the sovereign Zeus, who like a swan
Flies to fair-ankled Leda!

PANDORA.

Or perchance
Ixion's cloud, the shadowy shape of Hera,
That bore the Centaurs.

EPIMETHEUS.

The divine and human.

CHORUS OF BIRDS.

Gently swaying to and fro,
Rocked by all the winds that blow,
Bright with sunshine from above
Dark with shadow from below,
Beak to beak and breast to breast
In the cradle of their nest,
Lie the fledglings of our love.

ECHO

Love! love!

EPIMETHEUS.

Hark! listen! Hear how sweetly overhead
The feathered flute-players pipe their songs of love,
And echo answers, love and only love.

CHORUS OF BIRDS.

Every flutter of the wing,
Every note of song we sing,
Every murmur, every tone,
Is of love and love alone.

ECHO

Love alone!

EPIMETEHEUS.

Who would not love, if loving she might be
Changed like Callisto to a star in heaven?

PANDORA.

Ah, who would love, if loving she might be
Like Semele consumed and burnt to ashes?

EPIMETHEUS.

Whence knowest thou these stories?

PANDORA

Hermes taught me;
He told me all the history of the Gods.

CHORUS OF REEDS.

Evermore a sound shall be
In the reeds of Aready,
Evermore a low lament
Of unrest and discontent,
As the story is retold
Of the nymph so coy and cold,
Who with frightened feet outran
The pursuing steps of Pan.

EPIMETHEUS.

The pipe of Pan out of these reeds is made,
And when he plays upon it to the shepherds
They pity him, so mournful is the sound.
Be thou not coy and cold as Syrinx was.

PANDORA.

Nor thou as pan be rude and mannerless.

PROMETHEUS, *without.*

Ho! Epimetheus!

EPIMETHEUS.

'Tis my brother's voice;
A sound unwelcome and inopportune
As was the braying of Silenus' ass,
Heard in Cybele's garden.

PANDORA.

Let me go.
I would not be found here. I would not see him.

She escapes among the trees.

CHORUS OF DRYADES.

Haste and hide thee,
Ere too late,
In these thickets intricate;
Lest Prometheus
See and chide thee,
Lest some hurt
Or harm betide thee,
Haste and hide thee!

PROMETHEUS, *entering.*

Who was it fled from here? I saw a shape
Flitting among the trees.

EPIMETHEUS.

It was Pandora.

PROMETHEUS.

O Epimetheus! Is it then in vain
That I have warned thee? Let me now implore.
Thou harborest in thy house a dangerous guest.

EPIMETHEUS.

Whom the Gods love they honor with such guests.

PROMETHEUS.

Whom the Gods would destroy they first make mad.

EPIMETHEUS.

Shall I refuse the gifts they send to me?

PROMETHEUS.

Reject all gifts that come from higher powers.

EPIMETHEUS.

Such gifts as this are not to be rejected.

PROMETHEUS.

Make not thyself the slave of any woman.

EPIMETHEUS.

Make not thyself the judge of any man.

PROMETHEUS.

I judge thee not; for thou art more than man;
Thou art descended from Titanic race,
And hast a Titan's strength, and faculties
That make thee godlike; and thou sittest here
Like Heracles spinning Omphale's flax,
And beaten with her sandals.

EPIMETHEUS.

         O my brother!
Thou drivest me to madness with thy taunts.

PROMETHEUS.

And me thou drivest to madness with thy follies.
Come with me to my tower on Caucasus:
See there my forges in the roaring caverns,
Beneficent to man, and taste the joy
That springs from labor. Read with me the stars,
And learn the virtues that lie hidden in plants,
And all things that are useful.

EPIMETHEUS.

         O my brother!
I am not as thou art. Thou dost inherit
Our father's strength, and I our mother's weakness:
The softness of the Oceanides,
The yielding nature that cannot resist.

PROMETHEUS.

Because thou wilt not.

EPIMETHEUS.

Nay; because I cannot.

PROMETHEUS.

Assert thyself; rise up to thy full height;
Shake from thy soul these dreams effeminate,
These passions born of indolence and ease.
Resolve, and thou art free. But breathe the air
 Of mountains, and their unapproachable summits
Will lift thee to the level of themselves.

EPIMETHEUS.

The roar of forests and of waterfalls,
The rushing of a mighty wind, with loud
And undistinguishable voices calling,
Are in my ear!

PROMETHEUS.

O, listen and obey.

EPIMETHEUS.

Thou leadest me as a child. I follow thee.

They go out.

CHORUS OF OREADES.

Centuries old are the mountains;
Their foreheads wrinkled and rifted
Helios crowns by day,
Pallid Selene by night;
From their bosoms uptossed
The snows are driven and drifted,
Like Tithonus' beard
Streaming dishevelled and white.

Thunder and tempest of wind
Their trumpets blow in the vastness;
Phantoms of mist and rain,
Cloud and the shadow of cloud,
Pass and repass by the gates
Of their inaccessible fastness;
Ever unmoved they stand,
Solemn, eternal, and proud.

VOICES OF THE WATERS.

Flooded by rain and snow
In their inexhaustible sources,
Swollen by affluent streams
Hurrying onward and hurled
Headlong over the crags,
The impetuous water-courses,
Rush and roar and plunge
Down to the nethermost world.

Say, have the solid rocks.
Into streams of silver been melted,
Flowing over the plains,
Spreading to lakes in the fields?

Or have the mountains, the giants,
The ice-helmed, the forest-belted,
Scattered their arms abroad;
Flung in the meadows their shields?

VOICES OF THE WINDS.

High on their turreted cliffs
That bolts of thunder have shattered,
Storm-winds muster and blow
Trumpets of terrible breath;
Then from the gateways rush,
And before them routed and scattered
Sullen the cloud-rack flies,
Pale with the pallor of death.

Onward the hurricane rides,
And flee for shelter the shepherds;
White are the frightened leaves,
Harvests with terror are white;
Panic seizes the herds,
And even the lions and leopards,
Prowling no longer for prey,
Crouch in their caverns with fright.

VOICES OF THE FOREST.

Guarding the mountains around
Majestic the forests are standing,
Bright are their crested helms,
Dark is their armor of leaves;
Filled with the breath of freedom
Each bosom subsiding, expanding,
Now like the ocean sinks,
Now like the ocean upheaves.

Planted firm on the rock,
With foreheads stern and defiant,
Loud they shout to the winds,
Loud to the tempest they call;
Naught but Olympian thunders,
That blasted Titan and Giant,
Them can uproot and o'erthrow,
Shaking the earth with their fall.

CHORUS OF OREADES.

These are the Voices Three
Of winds and forests and fountains,
Voices of earth and of air,
Murmur and rushing of streams,
Making together one sound,
The mysterious voice of the mountains,
Waking the sluggard that sleeps,
Waking the dreamer of dreams.

These are the Voices Three,
That speak of endless endeavor,
Speak of endurance and strength,
Triumph and fulness of fame,
Sounding about the world,
An inspiration forever,
 Stirring the hearts of men,
 Shaping their end and their aim.

VII.

THE HOUSE OF EPIMETHEUS

PANDORA.

LEFT to myself I wander as I will,
And as my fancy leads me, through this house,
Nor could I ask a dwelling more complete
Were I indeed the Goddess that he deems me.
No mansion of Olympus, framed to be
The habitation of the Immortal Gods,
Can be more beautiful. And this is mine
And more than this, the love wherewith he crowns me.
As if impelled by powers invisible
And irresistible, my steps return
Unto this spacious hall. All corridors
And passages lead hither, and all doors
But open into it. Yon mysterious chest
Attracts and fascinates me. Would I knew
What there lies hidden! But the oracle
Forbids. Ah me! The secret then is safe.
So would it be if it were in my keeping.
A crowd of shadowy faces from the mirrors
That line these walls are watching me. I dare not
Lift up the lid. A hundred times the act
Would be repeated, and the secret seen
By twice a hundred incorporeal eyes.

She walks to the other side of the hall.

My feet are weary, wandering to and fro,
My eyes with seeing and my heart with waiting.
I will lie here and rest till he returns,
Who is my dawn, my day, my Helios.

Throws herself upon a couch, and falls asleep.

ZEPHYRUS.

Come from thy caverns dark and deep,
O son of Erebus and Night;
All sense of hearing and of sight
Enfold in the serene delight
And quietude of sleep!

Set all thy silent sentinels
To bar and guard the Ivory Gate,
And keep the evil dreams of fate
And falsehood and infernal hate
Imprisoned in their cells.

But open wide the Gate of Horn,
Whence, beautiful as planets, rise
The dreams of truth, with starry eyes,
And all the wondrous prophecies
And visions of the morn.

CHORUS OF DREAMS FROM THE IVORY GATE.

Ye sentinels of sleep,
It is in vain ye keep
Your drowsy watch before the Ivory Gate;
Though closed the portal seems,
The airy feet of dreams
Ye cannot thus in walls incarcerate.

We phantoms are and dreams
Born by Tartarean streams,
As ministers of the infernal powers;
O son of Erebus
And Night, behold! we thus
Elude your watchful wardens on the towers!

From gloomy Tartarus
The Fates have summoned us
To whisper in her ear, who lies asleep,
A tale to fan the fire
Of her insane desire
To know a secret that the Gods would keep.

This passion, in their ire,
The Gods themselves inspire,
To vex mankind with evils manifold,
So that disease and pain
O'er the whole earth may reign,
And nevermore return the Age of Gold.

PANDORA, *waking.*

A voice said in my sleep: "Do not delay:
Do not delay; the golden moments fly!
The oracle hath forbidden; yet not thee
Doth it forbid, but Epimetheus only!"
I am alone. These faces in the mirrors
Are but the shadows and phantoms of myself;
They cannot help nor hinder. No one sees me,
Save the all-seeing Gods, who, knowing good
And knowing evil, have created me
Such as I am, and filled me with desire
Of knowing good and evil like themselves.

She approaches the chest.

I hesitate no longer. Weal or woe,
Or life or death, the moment shall decide.

*She lifts the lid. A dense mist rises from the chest, and fills the
room. Pandora falls senseless on the floor. Storm without.*

CHORUS OF DREAMS FROM THE GATE OF HORN.

Yes, the moment shall decide!
It already hath decided;
And the secret once confided
To the keeping of the Titan
Now is flying far and wide,
Whispered, told on every side,
To disquiet and to frighten.

Fever of the heart and brain,
Sorrow, pestilence, and pain,
Moans of anguish, maniac laughter,
All the evils that hereafter
Shall afflict and vex mankind,
All into the air have risen
From the chambers of their prison;
Only Hope remains behind.

VIII.

IN THE GARDEN

EPIMETHEUS.

THE storm is past, but it hath left behind it
Ruin and desolation. All the walks
Are strewn with shattered boughs; the birds are silent;
The flowers, downtrodden by the wind, lie dead;
The swollen rivulet sobs with secret pain;
The melancholy reeds whisper together
As if some dreadful deed had been committed
They dare not name, and all the air is heavy
With an unspoken sorrow! Premonitions,
Foreshadowings of some terrible disaster
Oppress my heart. Ye Gods, avert the omen!

PANDORA, *coming from the house.*

O Epimetheus, I no longer dare
To lift mine eyes to thine, nor hear thy voice,
Being no longer worthy of thy love.

EPIMETHEUS.

What hast thou done?

PANDORA.

Forgive me not, but kill me.

EPIMETHEUS.

What hast thou done?

PANDORA.

I pray for death, not pardon.

EPIMETHEUS.

What hast thou done?

PANDORA.

I dare not speak of it.

EPIMETHEUS.

Thy pallor and thy silence terrify me!

PANDORA.

I have brought wrath and ruin on thy house!
My heart hath braved the oracle that guarded
The fatal secret from us, and my hand
Lifted the lid of the mysterious chest!

EPIMETHEUS.

Then all is lost! I am indeed undone.

PANDORA.

I pray for punishment, and not for pardon.

EPIMETHEUS.

Mine is the fault, not thine. On me shall fall
The vengeance of the Gods, for I betrayed
Their secret when, in evil hour, I said
It was a secret; when, in evil hour,
I left thee here alone to this temptation.
Why did I leave thee?

PANDORA.

    Why didst thou return?
Eternal absence would have been to me
The greatest punishment. To be left alone
And face to face with my own crime, had been
Just retribution. Upon me, ye Gods,
Let all your vengeance fall!

EPIMETHEUS.

    On thee and me.
I do not love thee less for what is done,
And cannot be undone. Thy very weakness
Hath brought thee nearer to me, and henceforth
My love will have a sense of pity in it,
Making it less a worship than before.

PANDORA.

Pity me not; pity is degradation.
Love me and kill me.

EPIMETHEUS.

      Beautiful Pandora!
Thou art a Goddess still!

PANDORA.

      I am a woman;
And the insurgent demon in my nature,
That made me brave the oracle, revolts
At pity and compassion. Let me die;
What else remains for me?

EPIMETHEUS.

      Youth, hope, and love:
To build a new life on a ruined life,
To make the future fairer than the past,
And make the past appear a troubled dream.
Even now in passing through the garden walks
Upon the ground I saw a fallen nest
Ruined and full of rain; and over me
Beheld the uncomplaining birds already
Busy in building a new habitation.

PANDORA.

Auspicious omen!

EPIMETHEUS.

> May the Eumenides
Put out their torches and behold us not,
And fling away their whips of scorpions
And touch us not.

PANDORA.

> Me let them punish.
Only through punishment of our evil deeds,
Only through suffering, are we reconciled
To the immortal Gods and to ourselves.

CHORUS OF THE EUMENIDES.

Never shall souls like these
  Escape the Eumenides,
The daughters dark of Acheron and Night!
  Unquenched our torches glare,
  Our scourges in the air
Send forth prophetic sounds before they smite.
  Never by lapse of time
  The soul defaced by crime.
Into its former self returns again;
  For every guilty deed
  Holds in itself the seed
Of retribution and undying pain.

Never shall be the loss
Restored, till Helios
Hath purified them with his heavenly fires;
Then what was lost is won,
And the new life begun,
Kindled with nobler passions and desires.

THE HANGING OF THE CRANE

52

THE HANGING OF THE CRANE

I.

THE lights are out, and gone are all the guests
That thronging came with merriment and jests
   To celebrate the Hanging of the Crane
In the new house, —into the night are gone;
But still the fire upon the hearth burns on,
   And I alone remain.

     O fortunate, O happy day,
     When a new household finds its place
     Among the myriad homes of earth,
     Like a new star just sprung to birth,
     And rolled on its harmonious way
     Into the boundless realms of space!

So said the guests in speech and song,
As in the chimney, burning bright,
We hung the iron crane to-night,
And merry was the feast and long.

II.

AND now I sit and muse on what may be,
And in my vision see, or seem to see,
    Through floating vapors interfused with light,
Shapes indeterminate, that gleam and fade,
As shadows passing into deeper shade
    Sink and elude the sight.

        For two alone, there in the hall,
        Is spread the table round and small;
        Upon the polished silver shine
        The evening lamps, but, more divine,
        The light of love shines over all;
        Of love, that says not mine and thine,
        But ours, for ours is thine and mine.

They want no guests, to come between
Their tender glances like a screen,
And tell them tales of land and sea,
And whatsoever may betide
The great, forgotten world outside;
They want no guests; they needs must be
Each other's own best company.

III.

THE picture fades; as at a village fair
A showman's views, dissolving into air,
   Again appear transfigured on the screen,
So in my fancy this; and now once more,
In part transfigured, through the open door
   Appears the selfsame scene.

     Seated, I see the two again,
     But not alone; they entertain
     A little angel unaware,
     With face as round as is the moon;
     A royal guest with flaxen hair,
     Who, throned upon his lofty chair,
     Drums on the table with his spoon,
     Then drops it careless on the floor,
     To grasp at things unseen before.

     Are these celestial manners? these
     The ways that win, the arts that please?
     Ah yes; consider well the guest,
     And whatsoe'er he does seems best;
     He ruleth by the right divine
     Of helplessness, so lately born
     In purple chambers of the morn,
     As sovereign over thee and thine.
     He speaketh not; and yet there lies
     A conversation in his eyes;
     The golden silence of the Greek,
     The gravest wisdom of the wise,
     Not spoken in language, but in looks
     More legible than printed books,
     As if he could but would not speak.
     And now, O monarch absolute,
     Thy power is put to proof; for, lo!

Resistless, fathomless, and slow,
The nurse comes rustling like the sea,
And pushes back thy chair and thee,
And so good night to King Canute.

IV.

As one who walking in a forest sees
A lovely landscape through the parted trees,
    Then sees it not, for boughs that intervene;
Or as we see the moon sometimes revealed
Through drifting clouds, and then again concealed,
    So I behold the scene.

There are two guests at table now;
The king, deposed and older grown,
No longer occupies the throne,—
The crown is on his sister's brow;
A Princess from the Fairy Isles,
The very pattern girl of girls,
All covered and embowered in curls,
Rose-tinted from the Isle of Flowers,
And sailing with soft, silken sails
From far-off Dreamland into ours.
Above their bowls with rims of blue
Four azure eyes of deeper hue
 Are looking, dreamy with delight ;
 Limpid as planets that emerge
 Above the ocean's rounded verge,
 Soft-shining through the summer night.
 Steadfast they gaze, yet nothing see
 Beyond the horizon of their bowls;
 Nor care they for the world that rolls
 With all its freight of troubled souls
 Into the days that are to be.

V.

AGAIN the tossing boughs shut out the scene,
Again the drifting vapors intervene,
    And the moon's pallid disk is hidden quite;
And now I see the table wider grown,
As round a pebble into water thrown
    Dilates a ring of light.

I see the table wider grown,
I see it garlanded with guests,
As if fair Ariadne's Crown
Out of the sky had fallen down;
Maidens within whose tender breasts
A thousand restless hopes and fears,
Forth reaching to the coming years,
Flutter awhile, then quiet lie,
Like timid birds that fain would fly,
But do not dare to leave their nests;—
And youths, who in their strength elate
Challenge the van and front of fate,
Eager as champions to be
In the divine knight-errantry
Of youth, that travels sea and land
Seeking adventures, or pursues,
Through cities, and through solitudes
Frequented by the lyric Muse,
The phantom with the beckoning hand,
That still allures and still eludes.
O sweet illusions of the brain!
O sudden thrills of fire and frost!
The world is bright while ye remain,
And dark and dead when ye are lost!

VI.

THE meadow-brook, that seemeth to stand still,
Quickens its current as it nears the mill;
    And so the stream of Time that lingereth
In level places, and so dull appears,
Runs with a swifter current as it nears
    The gloomy mills of Death.

And now, like the magician's scroll,
That in the owner's keeping shrinks
With every wish he speaks or thinks,
Till the last wish consumes the whole,
The table dwindles, and again
I see the two alone remain.
The crown of stars is broken in parts;
Its jewels, brighter than the day,
Have one by one been stolen away
To shine in other homes and hearts.
One is a wanderer now afar
In Ceylon or in Zanzibar,
Or sunny regions of Cathay;
And one is in the boisterous camp
Mid clink of arms and horses' tramp,
And battle's terrible array.
I see the patient mother read,
With aching heart, of wrecks that float
Disabled on those seas remote,
Or of some great heroic deed
On battle-fields, where thousands bleed
To lift one hero into fame.
Anxious she bends her graceful head
Above these chronicles of pain,
And trembles with a secret dread
Lest there among the drowned or slain
She find the one beloved name.

VII.

AFTER a day of cloud and wind and rain
Sometimes the setting sun breaks out again,
   And, touching all the darksome woods with light,
Smiles on the fields, until they laugh and sing,
Then like a ruby from the horizon's ring
   Drops down into the night.

What see I now? The night is fair,
The storm of grief, the clouds of care,
The wind, the rain, have passed away;
The lamps are lit, the fires burn bright,
The house is full of life and light:
It is the Golden Wedding day.
The guests come thronging in once more,
Quick footsteps sound along the floor,
The trooping children crowd the stair,
And in and out and everywhere
Flashes along the corridor
The sunshine of their golden hair.

On the round table in the hall
Another Ariadne's Crown
Out of the sky hath fallen down;
More than one Monarch of the Moon
Is drumming with his silver spoon;
The light of love shines over all.

O fortunate, O happy day!
The people sing, the people say.
The ancient bridegroom and the bride,
Smiling contented and serene
Upon the blithe, bewildering scene,
Behold, well-pleased, on every side
Their forms and features multiplied,

As the reflection of a light
Between two burnished mirrors gleams,
Or lamps upon a bridge at night
Stretch on and on before the sight,
Till the long vista endless seems.

MORITURI SALUTAMUS

POEMS

For the Fiftieth Anniversary of the
Class of 1825 in Bowdoin College

Tempora labuntur, tacitisque senescimus annis,
Et fugiunt freno non remorante dies.

OVID, *Fastorum*, Lib. vi.

MORITURI SALUTAMUS

"O CESAR, we who are about to die
Salute you!" was the gladiators' cry
In the arena, standing face to face
With death and with the Roman populace.

O ye familiar scenes, —ye groves of pine,
That once were mine and are no longer mine,—
Thou river, widening through the meadows green
To the vast sea, so near and yet unseen,—
Ye halls, in whose seclusion and repose
Phantoms of fame, like exhalations, rose
And vanished, —we who are about to die
Salute you; earth and air and sea and sky,
And the Imperial Sun that scatters down
His sovereign splendors upon grove and town.

Ye do not answer us! ye do not hear!
We are forgotten; and in your austere
And calm indifference, ye little care
Whether we come or go, or whence or where.
What passing generations fill these halls,
What passing voices echo from these walls,
Ye heed not; we are only as the blast,
A moment heard, and then forever past.

Not so the teachers who in earlier days
Led our bewildered feet through learning's maze;
They answer us —alas! what have I said?
What greetings come there from the voiceless dead?

What salutation, welcome, or reply?
What pressure from the hands that lifeless lie?
They are no longer here; they all are gone
Into the land of shadows, —all save one.
Honor and reverence, and the good repute
That follows faithful service as its fruit,
Be unto him, whom living we salute.

The great Italian poet, when he made
His dreadful journey to the realms of shade,
Met there the old instructor of his youth,
And cried in tones of pity and of ruth:
"O, never from the memory of my heart
Your dear, paternal image shall depart,
Who while on earth, ere yet by death surprised,
Taught me how mortals are immortalized;
How grateful am I for that patient care
All my life long my language shall declare."

To-day we make the poet's words our own,
And utter them in plaintive undertone;
Nor to the living only be they said,
But to the other living called the dead,
Whose dear, paternal images appear
Not wrapped in gloom, but robed in sunshine here;
Whose simple lives, complete and without flaw,
Were part and parcel of great Nature's law;
Who said not to their Lord, as if afraid,
"Here is thy talent in a napkin laid,"
But labored in their sphere, as men who live
In the delight that work alone can give.
Peace be to them; eternal peace and rest,
And the fulfilment of the great behest:
"Ye have been faithful over a few things,
Over ten cities shall ye reign as kings."

And ye who fill the places we once filled,
And follow in the furrows that we tilled,
Young men, whose generous hearts are beating high,
We who are old, and are about to die,
Salute you; hail you; take your hands in ours,
And crown you with our welcome as with flowers!
How beautiful is youth! how bright it gleams
With its illusions, aspirations, dreams!
Book of Beginnings, Story without End,
Each maid a heroine, and each man a friend!
Aladdin's Lamp, and Fortunatus' Purse,
That holds the treasures of the universe!
All possibilities are in its hands,
No danger daunts it, and no foe withstands;
In its sublime audacity of faith,
"Be thou removed!" it to the mountain saith,
And with ambitious feet, secure and proud,
Ascends the ladder leaning on the cloud!

As ancient Priam at the Scaan gate
Sat on the walls of Troy in regal state
With the old men, too old and weak to fight,
Chirping like grasshoppers in their delight
To see the embattled hosts, with spear and shield,
Of Trojans and Achaians in the field,
So from the snowy summits of our years
We see you in the plain, as each appears,
And question of you; asking, "Who is he
That towers above the others? Which may be
Atreides, Menelaus, Odysseus,
Ajax the great, or bold Idomeneus ? "

Let him not boast who puts his armor on
As he who puts it off, the battle done.
Study yourselves; and most of all note well

Wherein kind Nature meant you to excel.
Not every blossom ripens into fruit;
Minerva, the inventress of the flute,
Flung it aside, when she her face surveyed
Distorted in a fountain as she played;
The unlucky Marsyas found it, and his fate
Was one to make the bravest hesitate.

Write on your doors the saying wise and old,
"Be bold! be bold!" and everywhere —"Be bold;
Be not too bold!" Yet better the excess
Than the defect; better the more than less;
Better like Hector in the field to die,
Than like a perfumed Paris turn and fly.

And now, my classmates; ye remaining few
That number not the half of those we knew,
Ye, against whose familiar names not yet
The fatal asterisk of death is set,
Ye I salute! The horologe of Time
Strikes the half-century with a solemn chime,
And summons us together once again,
The joy of meeting not unmixed with pain.

Where are the others? Voices from the deep
Caverns of darkness answer me: "They sleep!"
I name no names; instinctively I feel
Each at some well-remembered grave will kneel,
And from the inscription wipe the weeds and moss,
For every heart best knoweth its own loss.

I see their scattered gravestones gleaming white
Through the pale dusk of the impending night;
O'er all alike the impartial sunset throws
Its golden lilies mingled with the rose;

We give to each a tender thought, and pass
Out of the graveyards with their tangled grass,
Unto these scenes frequented by our feet
When we were young, and life was fresh and sweet.

What shall I say to you? What can I say
Better than silence is? When I survey
This throng of faces turned to meet my own,
Friendly and fair, and yet to me unknown,
Transformed the very landscape seems to be;
It is the same, yet not the same to me.
So many memories crowd upon my brain,
So many ghosts are in the wooded plain,
I fain would steal away, with noiseless tread,
As from a house where some one lieth dead.
I cannot go; —I pause; —I hesitate;
My feet reluctant linger at the gate;
As one who struggles in a troubled dream
To speak and cannot, to myself I seem.

Vanish the dream! Vanish the idle fears!
Vanish the rolling mists of fifty years!
Whatever time or space may intervene,
I will not be a stranger in this scene.
Here every doubt, all indecision ends;
Hail, my companions, comrades, classmates, friends!

Ah me! the fifty years since last we met
Seem to me fifty folios bound and set
By Time, the great transcriber, on his shelves,
Wherein are written the histories of ourselves.
What tragedies, what comedies, are there;
What joy and grief, what rapture and despair!
What chronicles of triumph and defeat,
Of struggle, and temptation, and retreat!

What records of regrets, and doubts, and fears!
What pages blotted, blistered by our tears!
What lovely landscapes on the margin shine,
What sweet, angelic faces, what divine
And holy images of love and trust,
Undimmed by age, unsoiled by damp or dust!

Whose hand shall dare to open and explore
These volumes, closed and clasped forevermore?
Not mine. With reverential feet I pass;
I hear a voice that cries, "Alas! alas!
Whatever hath been written shall remain,
Nor be erased nor written o'er again;
The unwritten only still belongs to thee:
Take heed, and ponder well what that shall be."

As children frightened by a thunder-cloud
Are reassured if some one reads aloud
A tale of wonder, with enchantment fraught,
Or wild adventure, that diverts their thought,
Let me endeavor with a tale to chase
The gathering shadows of the time and place,
And banish what we all too deeply feel
Wholly to say, or wholly to conceal.

In mediæval Rome, I know not where,
There stood an image with its arm in air,
And on its lifted finger, shining clear,
A golden ring with the device, "Strike here!"
Greatly the people wondered, though none guessed
The meaning that these words but half expressed,
Until a learned clerk, who at noonday
With downcast eyes was passing on his way,
Paused, and observed the spot, and marked it well,
Whereon the shadow of the finger fell;

And, coming back at midnight, delved, and found
A secret stairway leading under ground.
Down this he passed into a spacious hall,
Lit by a flaming jewel on the wall;
And opposite in threatening attitude
With bow and shaft a brazen statue stood.
Upon its forehead, like a coronet,
Were these mysterious words of menace set:
"That which I am, I am; my fatal aim
None can escape, not even yon luminous flame!"

Midway the hall was a fair table placed,
With cloth of gold, and golden cups enchased
With rubies, and the plates and knives were gold,
And gold the bread and viands manifold.
Around it, silent, motionless, and sad,
Were seated gallant knights in armor clad,
And ladies beautiful with plume and zone,
But they were stone, their hearts within were stone;
And the vast hall was filled in every part
With silent crowds, stony in face and heart.

Long at the scene, bewildered and amazed
The trembling clerk in speechless wonder gazed;
Then from the table, by his greed made bold,
He seized a goblet and a knife of gold,
And suddenly from their seats the guests upsprang,
The vaulted ceiling with loud clamors rang,
The archer sped his arrow, at their call,
Shattering the lambent jewel on the wall,
And all was dark around and overhead;—
Stark on the floor the luckless clerk lay dead!

The writer of this legend then records
Its ghostly application in these words:

The image is the Adversary old,
Whose beckoning finger points to realms of gold;
Our lusts and passions are the downward stair
That leads the soul from a diviner air;
The archer, Death; the flaming jewel, Life;
Terrestrial goods, the goblet and the knife;
The knights and ladies, all whose flesh and bone
By avarice have been hardened into stone;
The clerk, the scholar whom the love of pelf
Tempts from his books and from his nobler self.

The scholar and the world! The endless strife,
The discord in the harmonies of life!
The love of learning, the sequestered nooks,
And all the sweet serenity of books;
The market-place, the eager love of gain,
Whose aim is vanity, and whose end is pain!

But why, you ask me, should this tale be told
To men grown old, or who are growing old?
It is too late! Ah, nothing is too late
Till the tired heart shall cease to palpitate.
Cato learned Greek at eighty; Sophocles
Wrote his grand Oedipus, and Simonides
Bore off the prize of verse from his compeers,
When each had numbered more than fourscore years,
And Theophrastus, at fourscore and ten,
Had but begun his Characters of Men.
Chaucer, at Woodstock with the nightingales,
At sixty wrote the Canterbury Tales;
Goethe at Weimar, toiling to the last,
Completed Faust when eighty years were past.
These are indeed exceptions; but they show
How far the gulf-stream of our youth may flow
Into the arctic regions of our lives,
Where little else than life itself survives.

As the barometer foretells the storm
While still the skies are clear, the weather warm,
So something in us, as old age draws near,
Betrays the pressure of the atmosphere.
The nimble mercury, ere we are aware,
Descends the elastic ladder of the air;
 The telltale blood in artery and vein
 Sinks from its higher levels in the brain;
Whatever poet, orator, or sage
May say of it, old age is still old age.
It is the waning, not the crescent moon,
The dusk of evening, not the blaze of noon:
It is not strength, but weakness; not desire,
But its surcease; not the fierce heat of fire,
The burning and consuming element,
But that of ashes and of embers spent,
In which some living sparks we still discern,
Enough to warm, but not enough to burn.

What then? Shall we sit idly down and say
The night hath come; it is no longer day?
The night hath not yet come; we are not quite
Cut off from labor by the failing light;
Something remains for us to do or dare;
Even the oldest tree some fruit may bear;
Not Oedipus Coloneus, or Greek Ode,
Or tales of pilgrims that one morning rode
Out of the gateway of the Tabard Inn,
But other something, would we but begin;
For age is opportunity no less
Than youth itself, though in another dress,
And as the evening twilight fades away
The sky is filled with stars, invisible by day.

BIRDS OF PASSAGE

Flight the Fourth.

CHARLES SUMNER

GARLANDS upon his grave,
    And flowers upon his hearse,
And to the tender heart and brave
    The tribute of this verse.

His was the troubled life,
    The conflict and the pain,
The grief, the bitterness of strife,
    The honor without stain.

Like Winkelried, he took
    Into his manly breast
The sheaf of hostile spears, and broke
    A path for the oppressed.

Then from the fatal field
    Upon a nation's heart
Borne like a warrior on his shield!—
    So should the brave depart.

Death takes us by surprise,
    And stays our hurrying feet;
The great design unfinished lies,
    Our lives are incomplete.

But in the dark unknown
    Perfect their circles seem,
Even as a bridge's arch of stone
    Is rounded in the stream.

Alike are life and death,
When life in death survives,
And the uninterrupted breath
Inspires a thousand lives.

Were a star quenched on high,
For ages would its light,
Still travelling downward from the sky,
Shine on our mortal sight.

So when a great man dies,
For years beyond our ken,
The light he leaves behind him lies
Upon the paths of men.

TRAVELS BY THE FIRESIDE

THE ceaseless rain is falling fast,
    And yonder gilded vane,
Immovable for three days past,
    Points to the misty main.

It drives me in upon myself
    And to the fireside gleams,
To pleasant books that crowd my shelf,
    And still more pleasant dreams.

I read whatever bards have sung
    Of lands beyond the sea,
And the bright days when I was young
    Come thronging back to me.

In fancy I can hear again
    The Alpine torrent's roar,
The mule-bells on the hills of Spain,
    The sea at Elsinore.

I see the convent's gleaming wall
    Rise from its groves of pine,
And towers of old cathedrals tall,
    And castles by the Rhine.

I journey on by park and spire,
    Beneath centennial trees,
Through fields with poppies all on fire,
    And gleams of distant seas.

I fear no more the dust and heat,
   No more I feel fatigue,
While journeying with another's feet
   O'er many a lengthening league.

Let others traverse sea and land,
   And toil through various climes,
I turn the world round with my hand
   Reading these poets' rhymes.

From them I learn whatever lies
   Beneath each changing zone,
And see, when looking with their eyes,
   Better than with mine own.

CADENABBIA

LAKE OF **C**OMO

No sound of wheels or hoof-beat breaks
    The silence of the summer day,
As by the loveliest of all lakes
    I while the idle hours away.

I pace the leafy colonnade
    Where level branches of the plane
Above me weave a roof of shade
    Impervious to the sun and rain.

At times a sudden rush of air
    Flutters the lazy leaves o'erhead,
And gleams of sunshine toss and flare
    Like torches down the path I tread.

By Somariva's garden gate
    I make the marble stairs my seat,
And hear the water, as I wait,
    Lapping the steps beneath my feet.

The undulation sinks and swells
    Along the stony parapets,
And far away the floating bells
    Tinkle upon the fisher's nets.

Silent and slow, by tower and town.
    The freighted barges come and go,
Their pendent shadows gliding down
    By town and tower submerged below.

The hills sweep upward from the shore,
   With villas scattered one by one
Upon their wooded spurs, and lower
   Bellaggio blazing in the sun.

And dimly seen, a tangled mass
   Of walls and woods, of light and shade,
Stands beckoning up the Stelvio Pass
   Varenna with its white cascade.

I ask myself, Is this a dream?
   Will it all vanish into air?
Is there a land of such supreme
   And perfect beauty anywhere?

Sweet vision! Do not fade away;
   Linger until my heart shall take
Into itself the summer day,
   And all the beauty of the lake.

Linger until upon my brain
   Is stamped an image of the scene,
Then fade into the air again,
   And be as if thou hadst not been.

MONTE CASSINO

TERRA DI LAVORO.

BEAUTIFUL Valley! through whose verdant meads
    Unheard the Garigliano glides along ;-
The Liris, nurse of rushes and of reeds,
    The river taciturn of classic song.

The Land of Labor and the Land of Rest,
    Where medieval towns are white on all
The hillsides, and where every mountain's crest
    Is an Etrurian or a Roman wall.

There is Alagna, where Pope Boniface
    Was dragged with contumely from his throne;
Sciarra Colonna, was that day's disgrace
    The Pontiff's only, or in part thine own?

There is Ceprano, where a renegade
    Was each Apulian, as great Dante saith,
When Manfred by his men-at-arms betrayed
    Spurred on to Benevento and to death.

There is Aquinum, the old Volscian town,
    Where Juvenal was born, whose lurid light
Still hovers o'er his birthplace like the crown
    Of splendor seen o'er cities in the night.

Doubled the splendor is, that in its streets
    The Angelic Doctor as a school-boy played,
And dreamed perhaps the dreams, that he repeats
    In ponderous folios for scholastics made.

And there, uplifted, like a passing cloud
   That pauses on a mountain summit high,
Monte Cassino's convent rears its proud
   And venerable walls against the sky.

Well I remember how on foot I climbed
   The stony pathway leading to its gate;
Above, the convent bells for vespers chimed,
   Below, the darkening town grew desolate.

Well I remember the low arch and dark,
   The courtyard with its well, the terrace wide,
From which far down the valley, like a park
   Veiled in the evening mists, was dim descried.

The day was dying, and with feeble hands
   Caressed the mountain tops; the vales between
Darkened; the river in the meadow-lands
   Sheathed itself as a sword, and was not seen.

The silence of the place was like a sleep,
   So full of rest it seemed; each passing tread
Was a reverberation from the deep.
   Recesses of the ages that are dead.

For, more than thirteen centuries ago,
   Benedict fleeing from the gates of Rome,
A youth disgusted with its vice and woe,
   Sought in these mountain solitudes a home.

He founded here his Convent and his Rule
   Of prayer and work, and counted work as prayer;
The pen became a clarion, and his school
   Flamed like a beacon in the midnight air.

What though Boccaccio, in his reckless way,
    Mocking the lazy brotherhood, deplores
The illuminated manuscripts, that lay
    Torn and neglected on the dusty floors?

Boccaccio was a novelist, a child
    Of fancy and of fiction at the best!
This the urbane librarian said, and smiled
    Incredulous, as at some idle jest.

Upon such themes as these, with one young friar
    I sat conversing late into the night,
Till in its cavernous chimney the wood-fire
    Had burnt its heart out like an anchorite.

And then translated, in my convent cell,
    Myself yet not myself, in dreams I lay;
And, as a monk who hears the matin bell,
    Started from sleep; already it was day.

From the high window I beheld the scene
    On which Saint Benedict so oft had gazed,—
The mountains and the valley in the sheen
    Of the bright sun, —and stood as one amazed.

Gray mists were rolling, rising, vanishing;
    The woodlands glistened with their jewelled crowns;
Far off the mellow bells began to ring
    For matins in the half-awakened towns.

The conflict of the Present and the Past,
    The ideal and the actual in our life,
As on a field of battle held me fast,
    While this world and the next world were at strife.

For, as the valley from its sleep awoke,
  I saw the iron horses of the steam
Toss to the morning air their plumes of smoke,
  And woke, as one awaketh from a dream.

AMALFI

SWEET the memory is to me
Of a land beyond the sea,
Where the waves and mountains meet,
Where, amid her mulberry-trees
Sits Amalfi in the heat,
Bathing ever her white feet.
In the tideless summer seas.

In the middle of the town,
From its fountains in the hills,
Tumbling through the narrow gorge,
The Canneto rushes down,
Turns the great wheels of the mills,
Lifts the hammers of the forge.

'Tis a stairway, not a street,
That ascends the deep ravine,
Where the torrent leaps between
Rocky walls that almost meet.
Toiling up from stair to stair
Peasant girls their burdens bear;
Sunburnt daughters of the soil,
Stately figures tall and straight,
What inexorable fate
Dooms them to this life of toil?

Lord of vineyards and of lands,
Far above the convent stands.
On its terraced walk aloof
Leans a monk with folded hands,

Placid, satisfied, serene,
Looking down upon the scene
Over wall and red-tiled roof;
Wondering unto what good end
All this toil and traffic tend,
And why all men cannot be
Free from care and free from pain,
And the sordid love of gain,
And as indolent as he.

Where are now the freighted barks
From the marts of east and west?
Where the knights in iron sarks
Journeying to the Holy Land,
Glove of steel upon the hand,
Cross of crimson on the breast?
Where the pomp of camp and court?
Where the pilgrims with their prayers?
Where the merchants with their wares,
And their gallant brigantines
Sailing safely into port
Chased by corsair Algerines?

Vanished like a fleet of cloud,
Like a passing trumpet-blast,
Are those splendors of the past,
And the commerce and the crowd!
Fathoms deep beneath the seas
Lie the ancient wharves and quays,
Swallowed by the engulfing waves ;
Silent streets and vacant halls,
Ruined roofs and towers and walls;
Hidden from all mortal eyes
Deep the sunken city lies:
Even cities have their graves!

This is an enchanted land!
Round the headlands far away
Sweeps the blue Salernian bay
With its sickle of white sand:
Further still and furthermost
On the dim discovered coast
Pæstum with its ruins lies,
And its roses all in bloom
Seem to tinge the fatal skies
Of that lonely land of doom.
On his terrace, high in air,
Nothing doth the good monk care
For such worldly themes as these.
From the garden just below
 Little puffs of perfume blow,
And a sound is in his ears
Of the murmur of the bees
In the shining chestnut-trees;
Nothing else he heeds or hears.
All the landscape seems to swoon
In the happy afternoon;
Slowly o'er his senses creep
The encroaching waves of sleep,
And he sinks as sank the town,
Unresisting, fathoms down,
Into caverns cool and deep!

Walled about with drifts of snow,
Hearing the fierce north-wind blow,
Seeing all the landscape white,
And the river cased in ice,
Comes this memory of delight,
Comes this vision unto me
Of a long-lost Paradise
In the land beyond the sea.

THE SERMON OF ST. FRANCIS

Up soared the lark into the air,
A shaft of song, a winged prayer,
As if a soul, released from pain,
Were flying back to heaven again.

St. Francis heard; it was to him
An emblem of the Seraphim;
The upward motion of the fire,
The light, the heat, the heart's desire.

Around Assisi's convent gate
The birds, God's poor who cannot wait,
From moor and mere and darksome wood
Came flocking for their dole of food.

"O brother birds," St. Francis said,
"Ye come to me and ask for bread,
But not with bread alone to-day
Shall ye be fed and sent away.

"Ye shall be fed, ye happy birds,
With manna of celestial words;
Not mine, though mine they seem to be,
Not mine, though they be spoken through me.

"O, doubly are ye bound to praise
The great Creator in your lays;
He giveth you your plumes of down,
Your crimson hoods, your cloaks of brown.

"He giveth you your wings to fly
And breathe a purer air on high,
And careth for you everywhere,
Who for yourselves so little care!"

With flutter of swift wings and songs
Together rose the feathered throngs,
And singing scattered far apart;
Deep peace was in St. Francis' heart.

He knew not if the brotherhood
His homily had understood;
He only knew that to one ear
The meaning of his words was clear.

BELISARIUS

I AM poor and old and blind;
The sun burns me, and the wind
    Blows through the city gate
And covers me with dust
From the wheels of the august
    Justinian the Great.

It was for him I chased
The Persians o'er wild and waste,
    As General of the East;
Night after night I lay
In their camps of yesterday;
    Their forage was my feast.

For him, with sails of red,
And torches at mast-head,
    Piloting the great fleet,
I swept the Afric coasts
And scattered the Vandal hosts,
    Like dust in a windy street.

For him I won again
The Ausonian realm and reign,
    Rome and Parthenope;
And all the land was mine
From the summits of Apennine
    To the shores of either sea.

For him, in my feeble age,
I dared the battle's rage,
    To save Byzantium's state,
When the tents of Zabergan,
Like snow-drifts overran
    The road to the Golden Gate.

And for this, for this, behold!
Infirm and blind and old,
    With gray, uncovered head,
Beneath the very arch
Of my triumphal march,
    I stand and beg my bread!

Methinks I still can hear,
Sounding distinct and near,
    The Vandal monarch's cry,
As, captive and disgraced,
With majestic step he paced,—
    "All, all is Vanity!"

Ah! vainest of all things
Is the gratitude of kings;
    The plaudits of the crowd
Are but the clatter of feet
At midnight in the street,
    Hollow and restless and loud.

But the bitterest disgrace
Is to see forever the face
    Of the Monk of Ephesus!
The unconquerable will
This, too, can bear; —I still
    Am Belisarius!

SONGO RIVER

NOWHERE such a devious stream,
Save in fancy or in dream,
Winding slow through bush and brake
Links together lake and lake.

Walled with woods or sandy shelf,
Ever doubling on itself
Flows the stream, so still and slow
That it hardly seems to flow.

Never errant knight of old,
Lost in woodland or on wold,
Such a winding path pursued
Through the sylvan solitude.

Never school-boy in his quest
After hazel-nut or nest,
Through the forest in and out
Wandered loitering thus about.

In the mirror of its tide
Tangled thickets on each side
Hang inverted, and between
Floating cloud or sky serene.

Swift or swallow on the wing
Seems the only living thing,
Or the loon, that laughs and flies
Down to those reflected skies.

Silent stream! thy Indian name
Unfamiliar is to fame;
For thou hidest here alone,
Well content to be unknown.

But thy tranquil waters teach
Wisdom deep as human speech,
Moving without haste or noise
In unbroken equipose.

Though thou turnest no busy mill,
And art ever calm and still,
Even thy silence seems to say
To the traveller on his way:—

"Traveller, hurrying from the heat
Of the city, stay thy feet!
Rest awhile, nor longer waste
Life with inconsiderate haste!

"Be not like a stream that brawls
Loud with shallow waterfalls,
But in quiet self-control
Link together soul and soul."

A BOOK OF SONNETS

THREE FRIENDS OF MINE

I.

When I remember them, those friends of mine,
    Who are no longer here, the noble three,
    Who half my life were more than friends to me,
    And whose discourse was like a generous wine,
I most of all remember the divine
    Something, that shone in them, and made us see
    The archetypal man, and what might be
    The amplitude of Nature's first design.
In vain I stretch my hands to clasp their hands;
    I cannot find them. Nothing now is left
    But a majestic memory. They meanwhile
Wander together in Elysian lands;
    Perchance remembering me, who am bereft
    Of their dear presence, and, remembering, smile.

II.

IN Attica thy birthplace should have been,
　　Or the Ionian Isles, or where the seas
　　Encircle in their arms the Cyclades,
　　So wholly Greek wast thou in thy serene
And childlike joy of life, O Philhelene!
　　Around thee would have swarmed the Attic bees;
　　Homer had been thy friend, or Socrates,
　　And Plato welcomed thee to his demesne.
For thee old legends breathed historic breath;
　　Thou sawest Poseidon in the purple sea,
　　And in the sunset Jason's fleece of gold!
O, what hadst thou to do with cruel Death,
　　Who wast so full of life, or Death with thee,
　　That thou shouldst die before thou hadst grown old!

III.

I STAND again on the familiar shore,
　　And hear the waves of the distracted sea
　　Piteously calling and lamenting thee,
　　And waiting restless at thy cottage door.
The rocks, the sea-weed on the ocean floor,
　　The willows in the meadow, and the free
　　Wild winds of the Atlantic welcome me;
　　Then why shouldst thou be dead, and come no more?
Ah, why shouldst thou be dead, when common men
　　Are busy with their trivial affairs,
　　Having and holding? Why, when thou hadst read
Nature's mysterious manuscript, and then
　　Wast ready to reveal the truth it bears,
　　Why art thou silent? Why shouldst thou be dead?

IV.

RIVER, that stealest with such silent pace
    Around the City of the Dead, where lies
    A friend who bore thy name, and whom these eyes
    Shall see no more in his accustomed place,
Linger and fold him in thy soft embrace
    And say good night, for now the western skies
    Are red with sunset, and gray mists arise
    Like damps that gather on a dead man's face.
Good night! good night! as we so oft have said
    Beneath this roof at midnight, in the days
    That are no more, and shall no more return.
Thou hast but taken thy lamp and gone to bed;
    I stay a little longer, as one stays
    To cover up the embers that still burn.

V.

THE doors are all wide open; at the gate
    The blossomed lilacs counterfeit a blaze,
    And seem to warm the air; a dreamy haze
    Hangs o'er the Brighton meadows like a fate,
And on their margin, with sea-tides elate,
    The flooded Charles, as in the happier days,
    Writes the last letter of his name, and stays
    His restless steps, as if compelled to wait.
I also wait; but they will come no more,
    Those friends of mine, whose presence satisfied
    The thirst and hunger of my heart. Ah me!
They have forgotten the pathway to my door!
    Something is gone from nature since they died,
    And summer is not summer, nor can be.

CHAUCER

AN old man in a lodge within a park;
    The chamber walls depicted all around
    With portraitures of huntsman, hawk, and hound,
    And the hurt deer. He listeneth to the lark,
Whose song comes with the sunshine through the dark
    Of painted glass in leaden lattice bound;
    He listeneth and he laugheth at the sound,
    Then writeth in a book like any clerk.
He is the poet of the dawn, who wrote
    The Canterbury Tales, and his old age
    Made beautiful with song; and as I read
I hear the crowing cock, I hear the note
    Of lark and linnet, and from every page
    Rise odors of ploughed field or flowery mead.

SHAKESPEARE

A VISION as of crowded city streets,
    With human life in endless overflow;
    Thunder of thoroughfares; trumpets that blow
    To battle; clamor, in obscure retreats,
Of sailors landed from their anchored fleets;
    Tolling of bells in turrets, and below
    Voices of children, and bright flowers that throw
    O'er garden-walls their intermingled sweets!
This vision comes to me when I unfold
    The volume of the Poet paramount,
    Whom all the Muses loved, not one alone;
Into his hands they put the lyre of gold,
    And, crowned with sacred laurel at their fount,
    Placed him as Musagetes on their throne.

MILTON

I PACE the sounding sea-beach and behold
   How the voluminous billows roll and run,
   Upheaving and subsiding, while the sun
   Shines through their sheeted emerald far unrolled,
And the ninth wave, slow gathering fold by fold
   All its loose-flowing garments into one,
   Plunges upon the shore, and floods the dun
   Pale reach of sands, and changes them to gold.
So in majestic cadence rise and fall
   The mighty undulations of thy song,
   O sightless bard, England's Mæonides!
And ever and anon, high over all
   Uplifted, a ninth wave superb and strong,
   Floods all the soul with its melodious seas.

KEATS

THE young Endymion sleeps Endymion's sleep;
    The shepherd-boy whose tale was left half told!
    The solemn grove uplifts its shield of gold
    To the red rising moon, and loud and deep
The nightingale is singing from the steep;
    It is midsummer, but the air is cold;
    Can it be death? Alas, beside the fold
    A shepherd's pipe lies shattered near his sheep.
Lo! in the moonlight gleams a marble white,
    On which I read: "Here lieth one whose name
    Was writ in water." And was this the meed
Of his sweet singing? Rather let me write:
    "The smoking flax before it burst to flame
    Was quenched by death, and broken the bruised reed."

THE GALAXY

TORRENT of light and river of the air,
   Along whose bed the glimmering stars are seen
  Like gold and silver sands in some ravine
   Where mountain streams have left their channels bare!
The Spaniard sees in thee the pathway, where
   His patron saint descended in the sheen
   Of his celestial armor, on serene
   And quiet nights, when all the heavens were fair.
Not this I see, nor yet the ancient fable
   Of Phaeton's wild course, that scorched the skies
   Where'er the hoofs of his hot coursers trod;
But the white drift of worlds o'er chasms of sable,
   The star-dust, that is whirled aloft and flies
   From the invisible chariot-wheels of God.

THE SOUND OF THE SEA

THE sea awoke at midnight from its sleep,
　　And round the pebbly beaches far and wide
　　I heard the first wave of the rising tide
　　Rush onward with uninterrupted sweep;
A voice out of the silence of the deep,
　　A sound mysteriously multiplied
　　As of a cataract from the mountain's side,
　　Or roar of winds upon a wooded steep.
So comes to us at times, from the unknown
　　And inaccessible solitudes of being,
　　The rushing of the sea-tides of the soul;
And inspirations, that we deem our own,
　　Are some divine foreshadowing and foreseeing
　　Of things beyond our reason or control.

A SUMMER DAY BY THE SEA

THE sun is set; and in his latest beams
    Yon little cloud of ashen gray and gold,
    Slowly upon the amber air unrolled,
    The falling mantle of the Prophet seems.
From the dim headlands many a lighthouse gleams,
    The street-lamps of the ocean; and behold,
    O'erhead the banners of the night unfold;
    The day hath passed into the land of dreams.
O summer day beside the joyous sea!
    O summer day so wonderful and white,
    So full of gladness and so full of pain!
Forever and forever shalt thou be
    To some the gravestone of a dead delight,
    To some the landmark of a new domain.

THE TIDES

I SAW the long line of the vacant shore,
　　The sea-weed and the shells upon the sand,
　　And the brown rocks left bare on every hand,
　　As if the ebbing tide would flow no more.
Then heard I, more distinctly than before,
　　The ocean breathe and its great breast expand,
　　And hurrying came on the defenceless land
　　The insurgent waters with tumultuous roar.
All thought and feeling and desire, I said,
　　Love, laughter, and the exultant joy of song
　　Have ebbed from me forever! Suddenly o'er me
They swept again from their deep ocean bed,
　　And in a tumult of delight, and strong
　　As youth, and beautiful as youth, upbore me.

A SHADOW

I SAID unto myself, if I were dead,
  What would befall these children? What would be
  Their fate, who now are looking up to me
  For help and furtherance? Their lives, I said,
Would be a volume wherein I have read
  But the first chapters, and no longer see
  To read the rest of their dear history,
  So full of beauty and so full of dread.
Be comforted; the world is very old,
  And generations pass, as they have passed,
  A troop of shadows moving with the sun;
Thousands of times has the old tale been told;
  The world belongs to those who come the last,
  They will find hope and strength as we have done.

A NAMELESS GRAVE

"A SOLDIER of the Union mustered out,"
    Is the inscription on an unknown grave
    At Newport News, beside the salt-sea wave,
    Nameless and dateless; sentinel or scout
Shot down in skirmish, or disastrous rout
    Of battle, when the loud artillery drave
    Its iron wedges through the ranks of brave
    And doomed battalions, storming the redoubt.
Thou unknown hero sleeping by the sea
    In thy forgotten grave! with secret shame
    I feel my pulses beat, my forehead burn,
When I remember thou hast given for me
    All that thou hadst, thy life, thy very name,
    And I can give thee nothing in return.

SLEEP

LULL me to sleep, ye winds, whose fitful sound
  Seems from some faint Æolian harpstring caught;
  Seal up the hundred wakeful eyes of thought
  As Hermes with his lyre in sleep profound
The hundred wakeful eyes of Argus bound;
  For I am weary, and am overwrought
  With too much toil, with too much care distraught,
  And with the iron crown of anguish crowned.
Lay thy soft hand upon my brow and cheek,
  O peaceful Sleep! until from pain released
  I breathe again uninterrupted breath!
Ah, with what subtile meaning did the Greek
  Call thee the lesser mystery at the feast
  Whereof the greater mystery is death!

THE OLD BRIDGE AT FLORENCE

TADDEO GADDI built me. I am old,
    Five centuries old. I plant my foot of stone
    Upon the Arno, as St. Michael's own
    Was planted on the dragon. Fold by fold
Beneath me as it struggles, I behold
    Its glistening scales. Twice hath it overthrown
    My kindred and companions. Me alone
    It moveth not, but is by me controlled.
I can remember when the Medici
    Were driven from Florence; longer still ago
    The final wars of Ghibelline and Guelf.
Florence adorns me with her jewelry;
    And when I think that Michael Angelo
    Hath leaned on me, I glory in myself.

IL PONTE VECCHIO DI FIRENZE

GADDI mi fece; il Ponte Vecchio sono;
    Cinquecent' anni già sull' Arno pianto
    Il piede, come il suo Michele Santo
    Piantò sul draco. Mentre ch' io ragiono
Lo vedo torcere con flebil suono
    Le rilucenti scaglie. Ha questi affranto
    Due volte i miei maggior. Me solo intanto
    Neppure muove, ed io non l'abbandono.
Io mi rammento quando fur cacciati
    I Medici; pur quando Ghibellino
    E Guelfo fecer pace mi rammento.
Fiorenza i suoi giojelli m' ha prestati;
    E quando penso ch' Agnolo il divino
    Su me posava, insuperbir mi sento.

ABOUT THE AUTHOR

Henry Wadsworth Longfellow (1807-1882) was an American poet and educator. His best-known original works include "Paul Revere's Ride," "The Song of Hiawatha" and "Evangeline." He was the first American to completely translate Dante Alighieri's "Divine Comedy" and was one of the fireside poets from New England.

Longfellow wrote many lyric poems known for their musicality and often presenting stories of mythology and legend. He became the most popular American poet of his day and had success overseas. He has been criticized for imitating European styles and writing poetry that was too sentimental.

1807

—February 27, 1807: Birth of Henry Wadsworth Longfellow at Portland, Maine (which was at that time still part of Massachusetts). He was the son of Stephen Longfellow, a lawyer, and Zilch Wadsworth, daughter of Peleg Wadsworth, a general in the American Revolutionary War and a member of Congress. His mother was descended from Richard Warren, who was a passenger on the Mayflower. His Mayflower ancestors also included William Brewster and John and Priscilla Alden.

1810

—Longfellow att4ends a dame school at age three.

1812

—April 30: Louisiana becomes the 18th state to j
—June 18: The War of 1812 begins, during which the United States of America and its indigenous allies fought against the United Kingdom and its allies in British North America.

1813

—Longfellow is enrolled at age six at the private Portland Academy.
—A naval battle occurs between American and British sips offshore of New England. The treaty restored diplomatic relations and restored the pre-war borders of June 1812.

1814

—December 24: The Treaty of Ghent, a peace treaty concluding the War of 1812, was signed at Ghent, in the Netherlands, by representatives of the United States and the United Kingdom.

1816

—The statehood of Indiana is recognized, and Indiana becomes the 19th state of the Union. Indiana had previously been part of the Northwest Territory organized in 1787.

1817

—December 10: Mississippi becomes the 20th state admitted to the Union of the United States. Mississippi seceded from the Union and was restored to the Union in 1870, after the American Civil War.

1818

—Illinois achieved statehood after being part of the Northwest

Territory for many years, becoming the 21st state of the Union.

1819

—December The statehood of Alabama is recognized. Alabama would later secede from the Union in 1861, rejoining the Union in 1868 after the American Civil War.

1820

—March 15: Maine becomes the 23rd state of the United States, as part of the Missouri Compromise, after residents voted to secede from the Commonwealth of Massachusetts.

—Longfellow's first poem, "The Battle of Lovell's Pond," was published in the Portland Gazette on November 17, 1820. It was a patriotic and historical four-stanza poem.

—Nathaniel Hawthorne enrolls at Bowdoin College.

1821

—The former Missouri Territory is admitted to the Union as a slave state as part of the Missouri Compromise. Although the Confederacy recognized Missouri as its twelfth state, the secession was disputed and later regarded as not in effect.

1822

—Longfellow enrolls at Bowdoin College in Brunswick, Maine, along with his brother Stephen. His grandfather was a founder of the college and his father was a trustee. Here he met Nathaniel Hawthorne, a lifelong friend.

1824

—Nearly 40 minor poems by Longfellow are published between January 1824 and his graduation in 1825, many of these at the short-lived Boston periodical, The United States Literary Gazette."

1825

—Longfellow graduates from Bowdoin College, fourth in his class and elected to Phi Beta Kappa. He gave the student commencement address.
—Longfellow is offered a job as professor of modern languages at his alma mater, on condition that he prepare by touring Europe and learning Romance languages.

1826

—January 30: Washington Irving, while living in Paris, is invited to travel to Madrid to inspect the Spanish archives in the library of the American consul.
—In May, Longfellow travels from New York to Le Havre, in France, aboard the ship 'Cadmus.' He spent three years in Europe, visiting France, Spain, Italy, Germany, and England. During his time abroad he learned French, Italian, Spanish, Portuguese, and German, mostly without formal instruction. While in Madrid, he met with Washington Irving, who encouraged his writing.
—July 4: Former U.S. Presidents Thomas Jefferson and John Adams both die on the 50th anniversary of the signing of the United States Declaration of Independence.

1827

—In the United Kingdom, George Canning succeeds Lord Liverpool as British prime minister.
—The term "socialist" is coined by Robert Owen in his London periodical, The Co-operative Magazine and Monthly Herald.

1828

—January: Washington Irving's book, "A History of the Life and Voyages of Christopher Columbus," was published.
—The first substantial praise of Longfellow's work is published, by John Neal, a fellow native of Portland, Maine, in the January 23, 1828 issue of his magazine, "The Yankee." He

wrote: "As for Mr. Longfellow, he has a fine genius and a pure and safe taste,…"

—December 3: Andrew Jackson is elected President of the United States, defeating incumbent John Quincy Adams.

1829

—March 22; Greece receives autonomy from the Ottoman Empire.

—July 23: In the United States, William Burt obtains the first patent for a form of typewriter, the typographer.

—In mid-August, Longfellow returns to the United States.

—August 27: Longfellow wrote to the president of Bowdoin that he was turning down the professorship because he considered the $600 salary "disproportionate to the duties required." The trustees raised his salary to $800 with an additional $100 to serve as the college's librarian, which required one hour of work per day. While teaching at the college he translated textbooks from French, Italian, and Spanish.

1831

—July 21: Leopold of Saxe-Coburg-Gotha is inaugurated as the first King of the Belgians in Brussels.

—September 14, Longfellow marries Mary Storer, a childhood friend from Portland, Maine.

1832

—February 28: Charles Darwin and the crew of HMS Beagle arrive at South America for the first time.

—Greece is recognized as a sovereign nation by the Treaty of Constantinople, ending the Greek War of Independence.

1833

—Washington Irving's book, "Tales of the Alhambra," a book of short stories, is published.

—Longfellow's first published book was a translation of poetry by the medieval Spanish poet, Jorge Manrique, "Coplas de Don Jorge Manrique."

—Publication of several nonfiction and fiction prose pieces inspired by Irving, including "The Indian Summer" and "The Bald Eagle."

1834

—Longfellow receives a letter from Harvard College offering him the Smith Professorship of Modern Languages, with the stipulation that he spend a year abroad. He and his wife travel to Europe, where he studies German as well as Dutch, Danish, Swedish, Finnish, and Icelandic.

—The Spanish Inquisition, which had begun in the 15th century, is suppressed by royal decree.

1835

—Publication of "Outer-Mer: A Pilgrimage Beyond the Sea," a collection of Prose works by Longfellow. The term "outer-mer" is French for "overseas."

—September 7: Charles Darwin arrives at the Galapagos Islands, aboard HMS Beagle.

—November 29: Death of Longfellow's first wife, after a miscarriage. Her body was shipped home to the United States for burial at Mount Auburn Cemetery near Boston.

—December 28: The Second Seminole War led by Osceola breaks out.

1836

—Longfellow returns to the United States and assumes the professorship at Harvard.

—June 15: Arkansas is the 25th state admitted into the United States of America. Arkansas seceded from the Union in 1861 and rejoined in 186, after the American Civil War.

—Sam Houston is elected as the first president of the Republic of Texas.

1837

—January 26: Michigan becomes the 26th state of the United States, following the Toledo War, a boundary dispute with Ohio, in which Ohio was granted the Toledo region and Michigan was given the western part of the Upper Peninsula.

—During the spring Longfellow has rented rooms at the Craigie House, built in 1759, which served as the headquarters of George Washington during the Siege of Boston. Previous boarders included Jared Sparks, Edward Everett, and Joseph Emerson Worcester. The house is preserved as the Longfellow House-Washington's Headquarters National Historic Site.

—Charles Dickens's "Oliver Twist" begins publication in serial form in London.

1838

—Longfellow writes the poem, "Footsteps of Angels," said to be about his late wife.

—June 28: The coronation of Queen Victoria takes place at Westminster Abbey in London.

—July 4: The Iowa Territory is formally established after a bill signed by U.S. President Martin Van Buren on June 12.

1839

—Publication of Longfellow's first poetry collection, "Voices of the Night," his first book of poetry. Although most of the book was translations, it included nine original poems and seven poems that he had written as a teenager.

—During Longfellow's seven-year long courtship of Frances "Fanny" Appleton, whose family lived at Beacon Hill in Boston. He often walked from Cambridge to the Appleton home by crossing the Boston Bridge. That bridge was replaced in 1906 with a new bridge later renamed as the Longfellow Bridge.

—Publication of "Hyperion: A Romance," a romance novel, whose main character, Paul Flemming, travels through Germany and falls in love with an Englishwoman who rejects him. The semi-autobiographical novel hints of his own travels, his atheistic beliefs and his own as yet unsuccessful courtship. The novel's descriptions of Germany would later inspire its use as a companion travel guide for American tourists in that country.

1840?

—Longfellow takes a six-month leave of absence from Harvard to attend a health spa in the former Marienberg Benedictine Convent at Boppard in Germany

1841

—Publication of Longfellow's "Ballads and Other Poems," which included "The Village Blacksmith" and "The Wreck of the Hesperus."
—January 26: Britain occupies Hong Kong, an island with a population of 7,500.
—March 4: William Henry Harrison is sworn in as the ninth President of the United States.
—April 6: John Tyler is sworn in as the tenth President of the United States, two days after Harrison's death of pneumonia.

1842

—Publication of the drama "The Spanish Student: A Play in Three Acts," a play in which he reflects on his time in Spain in the 1820s.
—Publication of Longfellow's "Poems on Slavery," his first public support of abolitionism and anti-slavery efforts. Most of the poems were written at sea in October 1842. The poems were later reprinted as anti-slavery tracts in 1843, and included: "To William E. Channing," "The Slave's Dream," "The Good Part," "The Slave in the Dismal Swamp," "The Slave

Singing at Midnight," "The Witnesses," "The Quadroon Girl," and "The Warning."

1843

—Longfellow marries Frances Elizabeth Appleton.
—Nathan Appleton, the father of Longfellow's wife, purchases the former Craigie house as a wedding present, and Longfellow lives there for the rest of his life.

1844

—Birth of Charles Appleton Longfellow
—Publication of "Poets and Poetry of Europe," with translations by Longfellow.

1845

—March 3: Florida is admitted to the Union as the 27th state. Florida, an area previously contested by Spain and Great Britain, had been ceded to the United States in 1819. Florida seceded from the Union in 1861 and rejoined in 1868, after the American Civil War.
—March 4: James K. Polk (1795-1849) is sworn in as the 11th president of the United States of America.
—Birth of Ernest Wadsworth Longfellow
—Publication of "The Belfry of Bruges and Other Poems," a poetry collection.
—Publication of "The Waif: A Collection of Poems," an anthology of poems by various authors, to which Longfellow contributed "Proem."
—December 29: Texas is recognized as the 28th state of the United States.

1846

—December 28, 1846: Iowa becomes the 29th state in the Union.

1847

—April 7: Birth of Fanny Longfellow, the Longfellows' first daughter. During childbirth, Dr. Nathan Cooley Keep administered ether to the mother as the first obstetric anesthetic in the United States.
—November 1: Publication of Longfellow's epic poem, "Evangeline: A Tale of Acadia."

1848

—May 29: Wisconsin becomes the 30th state to join the United States.

1849

—Publication of "Kavanagh: A Tale," a story of a country romance, in which Mr. Churchill, a school teacher, who has always planned to write a romance, but whose procrastination has never allowed him to start, until late in life he resigns himself to his "destiny."
—March 4: Major General Zachary Taylor (1784-1850) is sworn in as the 12th president of the United States of America.

1850

—Birth of Alice Mary Longfellow
—Publication of "The Seaside and the Fireside," a poetry collection.
—March 4: Millard Fillmore (1800-1874) is sworn in as the 13th president of the United States.

1851

—Publication of "The Golden Legend," a poem.

1852

—Publication of "The Poetical Works of Henry Wadsworth Longfellow," a poetry collection, in London, with illustrations by John Gilbert.

1853

—Birth of Edith Longfellow
—March 4: Franklin Pierce (1804-1869) is sworn in as the 14th president of the United States of America.
—June 13: Longfellow hosts a farewell dinner party at his Cambridge home for his friend Nathaniel Hawthorne, who was preparing to move overseas.

1854

—Longfellow retired from his teaching position at Harvard to focus on his writing

1855

—Birth of Anne Allegra Longfellow
—Publication of "The Song of Hiawatha," an epic poem in trochaic tetrameter, featuring Native American characters. The epic tells the fictional adventures of an Ojibwe warrior named Hiawatha and the tragedy of his love for Minnehaha, a Dakota woman.

1857

—March 4: James Buchanan (1791-1868) is sworn in as the 15th president of the United States of America.

1858

—May 11: The Minnesota Territory is admitted to the Union as the 32nd state in the United States.
—Publication of "The Courtship of Miles Standish and Other Poems," a poetry collection. "The Courtship of Miles Standish" is a narrative poem, written in dactylic hexameter, about the early days of Plymouth Colony, the colonial settlement established in America by the Mayflower pilgrims. The poem was among the most enduringly popular of Longfellow's works.

1859

—February 14: Oregon is admitted to the Union as the 33rd state of the United States.

—Longfellow is awarded an honorary doctorate of laws from Harvard.

1860

—April 6: Longfellow writes the poem, "Paul Revere's Ride," commemorating the actions of Paul Revere on April 18, 1775, when he was said to warn American patriot defenders of the approaching British, although not a historically accurate account. It was written the day after Longfellow visited the Old North Church in Boston and climbed its tower It was first published in the January 1861 issue of 'The Atlantic Monthly.' Longfellow's family was said to have a connection to the historical Paul Revere in that his maternal grandfather, Peleg Wadsworth, had been Revere's commander during the Penobscot Expedition.

1861

—January 29: Kansas becomes the 39th state to join the United States.

—March 4: Abraham Lincoln (1809-1865) is sworn in as the 16th president of the United States of America.

—April 12: Start of the American Civil War, in which the Union states and the states of the southern Confederacy fought over issues of slavery.

—July 9: Longfellow's wife was sealing an envelope with hot sealing wax, or lighting a match, when her dress caught fire and her body was badly burned.

—July 10: Death of Francis Appleton, Longfellow's wife.

—Death of Longfellow's second wife, after sustaining burns when her dress caught fire. The distraught Longfellow was himself was injured by burns on his face, after trying to quench the flames with his body, and after that wore a beard to conceal the scars.

1863

—January 1: The Emancipation Proclamation was a presidential proclamation and executive order issued by Abraham Lincoln granted freedom to the slaves of the Confederacy.

—June 20: West Virginia is admitted to the Union as the 35th state of the United States, after seceding from the Confederate State of Virginia.

—July 1-3: The Battle of Gettysburg, fought near the town of Gettysburg in Pennsylvania, in which Union forces halted the Confederates' invasion to the north, was considered a turning point of the American Civil War.

—Publication of "The Legend of Rabbi Ben Levi," a poem telling about Yehoshua ben Levi, a Jewish rabbi and scholar of the Talmud who lived in the land of Israel in the first half of the third century, and taught in the city of Lod, and was known for his debates of theological matters.

—November 23: Publication of "Tales of a Wayside Inn," a poetry collection, in which a group of people gathered at the Wayside Inn in Sudbury, Massachusetts, (about 20 miles from the poet's home in Cambridge), each take turns each telling a story in a variety of poetic forms and styles. The characters are said to be loosely based on actual persons of Longfellow's acquaintance. Includes his previously published poem, "Paul Revere's Ride," and "The Saga of King Olaf." Includes the "second flight" of "Birds of Passage").

—December 25: Longfellow writes the poem "Christmas Bells," which becomes the lyrics of the beloved Christmas carol, "I Heard the Bells on Christmas Day."

1864

—Longfellow launches the "Dante Club," of friends who meet weekly to help with perfecting the translation of Dante Alighieri's "Divine Comedy." Guests included regulars

William Dean Howells, James Russell Lowell, and Charles
Eliot Norton.

—October 31: Nevada becomes the 36th state of the Union.

1865

—Longfellow's poem, "Christmas Bells," is published in "Our
Young Folks," a juvenile magazine published by Ticknor
and Fields.

—Publication of "Household Poems," a poetry collection.

—April 9: Confederate General Robert E. Lee surrenders to Union
General Ulysses S. Grant after the Battle of Appomattox
Court House.

—April 15: Andrew Johnson (1808-1875) is sworn in as the 17th
president of the United States of America, following the
assassination of Abraham Lincoln.

1867

—March 1: Nebraska becomes the 37th state of the Union.

—Publication of "The Divine Comedy," Longfellow's translation
of Dante Alighieri's work, in three volumes, although revi-
sions continued and the work went through four printings
in the first year.

—Publication of "Flower-de-Luce," a poetry collection.

1868

—Publication of "The New England Tragedies," containing two
dramatic plays in verse reflecting on events in the early
days of New England. The play "John Endicott" dramatizes
the clash between the Puritans and the Quakers and the
play "Giles Corey of the Salem Farms" is about the Salem
witchcraft trials.

1869

—March 4: General Ulysses S. Grant (1822-1885) is sworn in as the
18th president of the United States of America.

1871

—Publication of Longfellow's translation of Dante Alighieri's "The Divine Tragedy," in three volumes.

1872

—Publication of "Christus: A Mystery," a trilogy composed of three previous works: "The Golden Legend," The New England Tragedies," and "The Divine Tragedy."
—Publication of "Three Books of Song," a poetry collection (including the second part of "Tales of a Wayside Inn").
—Longfellow's poem, "Christmas Bells," is set to music by the English organist, John Baptiste Calkin, using a melody called "Waltham." Other melodies have been used, including the 1845 melody of "Mainzer" and a 1956 tune by Johnny Marks, which was popularized by a Bing Crosby recording.

1873

—Publication of "Aftermath," (comprising the third part of "Tales of a Wayside Inn," and the "third flight" of "Birds of Passage").

1874

—Samuel Ward helped Longfellow with the selling of a poem, "The Hanging of the Crane," to the 'New York Ledger' for $3,000, the highest price ever paid for a poem.
—Longfellow oversees the publication of a 31-volume anthology, called "Poems of Places," which collected poems representing geographical locations, including European, Asian, and Arabian countries.

1875

—Publication of "The Masque of Pandora and Other Poems," a poetry collection.

1876

—August 1: Colorado is admitted to the Union, after being organized as the Territory of Colorado since 1861.

1877

—March 4: Rutherford B. Hayes (1822-1893) is sworn in as the 19th president of the United States of America.

1878

—Publication of "Kêramos and Other Poems," a poetry collection.

1880

—Publication of "Ultima Thule," a poetry collection.

1881

—March 4: James A. Garfield ((1831-1881) is sworn in as the 20th president of the United States of America.

1882

—March 24: Death of Longfellow at his home in Cambridge, surrounded by family. He is buried at Mount Auburn Cemetery in Cambridge, Massachusetts.
—Publication of "In the Harbor," a poetry collection.

—Publication of "Michael Angelo: A Fragment," (incomplete, published posthumously).